To all of us and our beautiful,
endangered yet so alive world

Love yes, extinction no, embracing being alive... I guess we're all, day by day, looking to find or open a way in life. For me that includes looking for words that reach you. I wonder how you may feel as you read this. I communicate with myself while communicating with you. We're each on this planet facing our lives and the life of our world. How do we live in a way that is both personal and planetary? How can we feel growingly alive and make life better?

Among other things, words can maybe breathe life? I once attempted and came close to suicide, and we humans could be close to global suicide. Yet here now, I'm alive, we're alive, our world is alive ... I have chronic illness: at the time of writing, I've been bedbound for years; people assist with my care, linking me with the human community on our planet. And through my window I see trees and hear birds, linking me with the wider community of life on Earth. A community of life mortally at risk - yet alive ... and healable, surely? Within me, 'contradictory' emotions somehow link together in caring about our community of life ... grief, joy ... urgency, peace ... vulnerability, wonder. And amid widespread devastation on Earth, I encounter in my own painful feelings of devastation something paradoxical - unfathomable - warm, wondrous and well: a growing sense of possibility that we can survive, thrive, really alive - individually and collectively - saving and healing our world. Caring about this opens me to our vulnerability and strength facing personal and planetary life. The fabric of life, woven with uncountable threads, links me and you ... as I write and you read. Here we are. With our differences and with things in common. Our differences and common ground create a relationship. You and I and We?

In all this, I'm finding I need to open myself to a loving wholeness of being - however 'imperfectly' - embracing both the practical and the transcendent. At a transcendent level of love, I'm a being among beings within maybe universal being(s). At a practical level of love, this means giving my attention three-ways: me, community with others (including with you through this book), and planet. When I only focus on 'me', I actually lose myself - a kind of gradual personal inner extinction or living death ... alongside the accelerating mass extinction of species out in the world. Equally, if I just focus on 'the planet' or 'community' and sacrifice myself - same result: painful-yet-numbing inner living death. Put simply, if I ignore any of the three ... same result. I need all three. I need to say no to extinction, whether an incremental inner living death of me, or a dying sense of community, or mass extinction of species - including human extinction ... ultimately extinction of life on Earth - extinction of a living planet.

As best I can, I write things the way I experience them. Often the things I experience can be expressed as a kind of combined statement-and-question - a 'maybe'. Or plural 'maybes'. I offer you my maybes, for you perhaps to contemplate and see if they in some way chime with your maybes. Maybes are possibilities. As you, I, and all of us explore where our maybes meet, we can perhaps together create unfolding possibilities - unfolding realities - for us to survive, thrive, be really alive while saving and healing our world. Maybe it can all mean saying yes to love, however 'imperfectly' yet however we can … feeling growingly alive and making life better? The chapters of this book lay out some realities as well as some maybes that could be real possibilities:

1. Alive

Extinction - whether gradual inner living death, or a dying sense of community, or the potentially apocalyptic mass extinction started by humans - fills me with a kind of despair or dread which somehow is also hope and purpose: maybe these interconnected types of extinction can be stopped by love? Ok, there's plenty in me and the world that isn't love, yet there is love in our world, in us, in me. Maybe love is already healing our planet ... I'm exploring - come with me if you like? So many species are going extinct, and humans could too. When I am not numb to it, this unfolding tragedy fills me with, yes, despair and dread - yet love seems to embrace this felt vulnerability as a channel for purpose, action, hope. I can participate with others - for myself, for others, for our world. We are all part of life on Earth, under threat yet alive. There are maybe real possibilities for personal, local, global healing?

love yes, extinction no, embracing being

2. Ally

Aliveness opposes extinction - screams "No!", whispers "no", gives a silent no, to extinction. Yet aliveness in our times needs an ally. Maybe the ally is love. Love brings together my furious "No!", my determined "no", my trusting no...

Extinguishing life is one type of extinction. As can be extinguishing hope, extinguishing individual identity, extinguishing culture and community - all these are alive and resist extinction. Maybe love can prevent such tragic extinctions, through healing. Some extinctions happen naturally, as part of life. Not so, most human-induced extinctions - whether of species, or of lives, hopes, identities, communities. I nearly succumbed to self-induced extinction, but my aliveness, allied with love I believe, saved me. (More on that as this book unfolds.) Maybe love makes us more alive?

Iyeneba

3. Save

I'm glad and fortunate to be alive. On my 50th birthday, in a terrible crisis of desperation, I tried to take my own life, and came close to dying, yet in the end it was me that saved my life, with the help of others. "I don't want to die in so much pain," I thought - or felt - as my choosing to die became my choosing to stay alive.

I was so weak from my suicide attempt that I only just managed to make it to the phone to call an ambulance.

Maybe we humans are feeling the pain of potential collective suicide by extinction - the pain telling us we really do want to survive, thrive, be alive, now and through future generations ... we really do want to save our world. This pain is maybe, little by little, being melted in a warm, purposeful aliveness of love and healing?

love yes, extinction no, embracing being

4. Care

I experience within myself a mix of love and unlove. My unlove doesn't make me 'bad'. I see it as a kind of illness - which needs to be met, not with blame and punishment, but with compassion, clarity and care.

During much of my life, unlove-illness has come close to destroying me in many different ways. Yet in the moment of averting suicide - when I was choosing life over death - love was increasing a little, unlove reducing a little, unlove-illness healing a little. I cared about my pain. I wanted to die in a more self-caring way. Fourteen years later, I'm alive.

Unlove-illness pulls humanity towards extinction ... Maybe love is offering us care to sustain life?

lyeneba

5. Possibility

With chronic illness, I'm very limited in what I can do. These limitations, however, go hand-in-hand with possibilities. So my sometimes painful frustration at what I can't do, is relieved by appreciation and pleasure at what I can do. I can play my part alongside others playing their part ... maybe we can do what we truly desire, what we truly love, what we (and our world) truly need to survive, thrive, be really alive. We can each contribute to a healing of unlove-illness through growing love. None of us has to do it all! I, for example, can write this small book. At the moment I can't manage a longer book. That's ok. Maybe the brevity can be a strength. We can each do what is possible - without overburdening ourselves - and all our possibilities could add up to stopping extinction, inwardly and outwardly. Maybe we can feel good about life, while saving and healing our world?

love yes, extinction no, embracing being

6. Vital

Fourteen years ago, I had cut my wrists. My vital signs were so low that the ambulance crew put me on oxygen and a rapid drip for a while, before moving me. I was quivering with life-and-death, terrified, and so glad for their help.

As our planet Earth's vital signs plummet, so too are the vital signs of the human species. Yet we have the capacity to be the ambulance crew for our species, as well as other species and our world. We have the know-how, the technology, the skill. Maybe all we need is the love that gradually heals unlove-illness and stops unlove - the love that is maybe already growing in our world.

Love is vital - and gives us vitality - for us and our world to survive, thrive, be really alive. Our world could die from unlove. As we face this, maybe we can indeed be alive with love - and keep our world alive ... with love?

Iyeneba

7. Roots

What are the roots of the human self-destructiveness that could destroy our world? And what have been the roots of my own self-destructiveness that almost destroyed me?

In me, there have been many roots - all linked by pain. This pain, while it can drive self-destruction, can also open into healing. Pain needs love, compassion and care. Yet pain is often met by unlove. It is unlove-illness that turned my pain into self-destructiveness - whereas love progressively heals my pain into growing aliveness.

By tracing the path of my pain, love gradually unravels the roots, allowing them to drink life (rather than soak up destruction).

Maybe our world can drink life?

love yes, extinction no, embracing being

8. Transfusion

At the hospital, after tests I was told the loss of blood had hit my kidneys. "You have absolute renal failure," the emergency doctor said with a flash of anger. I felt mortified. Today, looking back, I feel compassion for the two of us - a doctor and a suicide survivor thrown together amid the life-and-death realities of a hospital.

"This was clearly a serious suicide attempt," another doctor said, kindly - adding that my kidneys would probably recover but I needed to be kept in hospital for monitoring. Over the next few days I was put on a drip for hydration, as well as being given blood transfusions.

Maybe the life-support systems of Earth can recover, with monitoring and a transfusion of care?

lyeneba

9. Choosing

We have choices - yet in certain ways none of us has a choice. I had no choice about the family and society I was born into. I didn't choose the tragic history of unlove that caused damage and suffering down the generations before me - and was passed on to me in my early life. None of us chose the planetary and human evolutionary history that has led to this moment of accelerating mass extinction. Yet there was, and is, love too. The lights and shadows of love down the generations haven't been obliterated by the toxic fog of unlove. The contours of the land are visible, and pathways can be chosen?

Maybe - imperfectly yet growingly - we can choose a path of healing. Maybe there is already a growing transformation underway of deadly unlove into aliveness with love?

love yes, extinction no, embracing being

10. Bridging

The legacy of unlove I received in my formative years, also interacted with genes and culture. This triad of nurture, nature and culture - along with other factors perhaps - caused unlove-illness in me. I suffered as others had suffered before me. The hurts and wounds of the past unleashed new hurts and wounds. Damage and destructiveness towards self and others - subtle or extreme - proliferated, disrupting inner bridges within myself, and outer bridges with others and the world. My suicide attempt nearly blew the final bridge, but somehow, thank goodness, that teetering bridge just survived as I chose life and got to the phone.

Maybe our inner and outer bridges are being restored. Maybe we can be part of love's wider bridging within and between humans - and with other living beings and our planet ... and...?

Iyeneba

11. Degrees

There are degrees of unlove. It can be subtle, barely perceptible. It can be extreme, horrific. It can be anywhere on a spectrum. Whatever the degree, unlove deadens aliveness.

Love restores aliveness - makes me more alive. Unlove has sometimes given an illusion of making me more alive, but in reality it has always depleted life-energy, making me less alive - prompting an ongoing day-by-day living death, degree by degree. Yet love offers an ongoing day-by-day way of really living?

Love seeks out the pain that underlies unlove, gradually healing wounds and distortions, giving greater freedom. Maybe the personal and collective pain behind the unlove driving mass extinction is healing, degree by degree ... increasingly opening into a freer, more alive, more loving world for us all?

love yes, extinction no, embracing being

12. Better

After my suicide attempt, once the emergency hospital had stabilised my physical state, I was in psychiatric hospital for 20 months.

I was dealing with a combination of severe chronic illness sapping my body and severe mental health difficulties from my childhood experiences, plus whatever else. My desperation from this had driven my attempt to take my own life. My experience in psychiatric hospital was mixed - at times good, at times not good - but the main thing is, the hospital did keep me alive. For that I'm thankful. A gateway opened for me to build a better life.

Earth and humanity are in a health crisis - physical, mental and existential. Maybe we can keep our world alive, and build a better life for all?

Iyeneba

13. Difference

We are all different. My story isn't the same as yours. Yet we share one planet. Our differences enrich our world. Each of us plays a part - within the interrelated parts that together we play on Earth.

Not only are we all different, each of us also makes a difference - in our own lives, in the lives of others, and in the life of our world.

I feel sad that the difference I've made has at times been unloving - for the worse, not the better, whether for me or others. I'm glad that with healing, I can growingly make a loving difference for me and others - in collaboration with all who are making their loving difference. Not perfectly. Unlove doesn't disappear, but it lessens, as love maybe makes the immeasurable difference?

love yes, extinction no, embracing being

14. Repair

I was unkind and sharp with a carer recently, and afterwards felt regret and sadness about the unlove. The next time I saw her, I sensed she was withdrawn and hurt. And I, too, had been hurt by my unlove. I told her I was sorry. We talked about it. She said, yes, in her view I had been sharp, and she had felt hurt. She was glad for the apology. The strain between us softened into warmth. We smiled. And soon we had a laugh about something or other. There was repair for each of us, and for our relationship.

Where unlove damages, love can repair - personally, locally, globally. Repair opens more aliveness with love. In our interconnected world, any repair helps other repairs - they accumulate - maybe in an inner and outer healing of ourselves and our planet?

Iyeneba

15. Distinguishing

Sometimes I find it hard to distinguish unlove from love - they can seem to blur. In a given situation, both may be present. In fact, I don't think I've ever experienced pure love. I need to compassionately accept I'm human - I'm not a love-robot! The main thing is, I'm gradually distinguishing better. I can find ways to move the dial a bit further - from unlove to love. I'm also glad I can learn from - and with - others. We learn together as well as individually.

Perhaps we humans, for all our self-destructive tendencies, are overall getting better at distinguishing unlove from love - and better at moving the dial away from extinction towards a healing world. Although sometimes things can seem to be getting worse, maybe love is growing more than unlove, for the better?

love yes, extinction no, embracing being

16. Naming

At the start of my life, I was given a name different to my name now. After my suicide attempt, I needed an identity that could help me heal from childhood damage. I changed my legal name by deed poll - to balance separation from, yet connection with, my parents and ancestors - separating from their unlove, yet connecting with their love. The letters of my new last name are: M, which has many meanings for me, affirming my individuality distinct from ancestry; JACMBR, the initial letters of my parents' and grandparents' first names; and AO, for 'All Other' ancestors. And I chose 'Seb' because I liked it. I'm not suggesting everyone change their name! But for me, it helped.

Language counts - it is a truly wondrous instrument - and maybe it can evolve in our journey of healing unlove-illness with love?

Iyeneba

17. Seeds

Love doesn't reject the unlove-ill parts of me; love is gradually healing them. Within any unlove, there lies a potential seed of love. It may be damaged and distorted - at times severely - even seemingly beyond rehabilitation ... yet love compassionately embraces every part of me, however sick with unlove, for healing. Hatred, for example, has been shifting away from hatred of myself and others, to hatred of unlove itself - combined with growing compassion for unlove-illness, whether in me or others. A sense of purpose.

Increasingly, love tends and heals the wounds, defuses the destructiveness towards self and others, stops the harm - uncovering seeds of recovery bit by bit, seeds of love. As unlove-illness heals, unlove can morph into love in our world. Everywhere are seeds, green shoots, new examples maybe of burgeoning love, burgeoning aliveness?

love yes, extinction no, embracing being

18. Rhythm

There are small rhythms of a day, a week, a month - and larger rhythms of a year, a decade, a century, a millennium ... Can we live small daily rhythms of wellbeing in our lives, while also living the great rhythms of this era? - an era of extreme challenge for our human role on Earth.

For me, small - even moment-by-moment - rhythms have a big impact on my quality of life with chronic illness. Rhythms of breathing, sleep, activity, rest, food, human contact, alone time, nature, creativity, work, play, leisure, and so on. Unlove causes mis-rhythms, damaging to wellbeing. When I notice this, I can open myself to more loving rhythms - I feel better.

Our personal rhythms can maybe interweave with collective human and planetary rhythms of healing our world?

lyeneba

19. Well

So many meanings of 'well'.

We can be well. We can do things well.

We can draw on the deep well of love. Love can well up inside us.

We may well have no answer to a problem. Yet we may be well resourced to find it.

We may feel well or unwell. Or both together, paradoxically - for instance in the mix of love and unlove. Maybe we can get less unwell, more well, as unlove-illness heals with love.

Love is well - compassionately well - so even with chronic illness, I can somehow also be well in life.

Can we make our ill world well? Well, I guess it's up to us. Well, well, well...?!

love yes, extinction no, embracing being

20. Way

As a species, having lost our way, we humans are maybe beginning to find our way again. The tragedy of incremental mass extinction has become a sign of our lostness, yet also an opportunity for us to face reality and find ourselves. Many of us had become cut off from our planet and other living beings - cut off in unlove-illness ... so cut off that we didn't fully realise the accelerating danger from our old way of life - but now increasingly we do realise, and we have a shot at a new way of life. A shot at healing unlove-illness, through a growing love - for ourselves, each other, and the living beings we share this planet with. I'm part of all this ... I'm given a way to heal from unlove - to be happier, along with all my feelings, through love.

Along with all our feelings, through love we have a way maybe to be happier than we ever were?

Iyeneba

21. Story

I've been telling you parts of my story. And parts of your own story may come to you as you read. We all have our individual stories. And we also have a shared story. The story of humanity, the wider story of life on Earth, the story of our cosmos...

We have the opportunity not only to have a story and tell our story, but also together create maybe the loveliest story of our time - how we faced unlove-illness and mass extinction, how with more love we began to heal ourselves and our world, how we gave a better planet to future generations - for them to continue the growing transformation of deadly unlove into aliveness with love - as we and our descendants saved life on Earth, saved humans and other Earth beings, and journeyed into the cosmos maybe not as death-dealers but life-givers?

love yes, extinction no, embracing being

22. With

I'm here on Earth with others, whether human or non-human. Interconnected and interdependent. My unlove-illness either blocks 'with' and my sense of community, or at the other extreme inflates 'with' into pseudo-community denying individuality. Either way, unlove deadens the aliveness of real relating, inwardly with myself, outwardly with others (and beyond inner/outer?) Unlove-illness fractures our world, causing needless suffering and needless death, hastening inner and outer extinction, through inner living death, outer dying community, and mass extinction. It perpetuates devastating conflicts that are bleeding our world, potentially to death. Love creates real 'with' - an alive feeling of connection - showing that my conflicts aren't *against* others or myself, but *with* others and myself. This *with* in our world is maybe a path to a healing resolution for each and all?

Iyeneba

23. Reality

Love is real. My unlove-illness distorts reality, especially when unlove gives an illusion of being 'realistic'. Love has realistic ideals. Reality can be hard. Sometimes love makes hard choices. If a person is about to kill others, the only way to save those lives - the loving choice - may be to kill the potential killer. In extreme untreatable suffering, especially with terminal illness, some may lovingly kill themselves. Love kills reluctantly but necessarily. Unlove kills indiscriminately and needlessly - sometimes directly, but often indirectly, for example when neglect leads sooner or later to death. The horror of unlove is real; love faces this horror, seeks a way to stop it and heal the unlove-illness behind it.

As my unlove-illness heals, I can growingly feel alive in love's reality. And together maybe we can be really alive in love's realities on Earth?

love yes, extinction no, embracing being

24. Climate

The climate crisis on Earth results from the human societal climate. I can't control the human societal climate, but I can participate in healing with others. This healing allows my personal micro-climate to shift, bit by bit, out of unlove into more love, alongside others whose personal micro-climates are shifting also. Together, our micro-climates can connect in broader climates of community healing - while communities around the planet can connect in a worldwide community of climate healing on Earth.

I can focus on my inner climate as I heal within, and my outer climate as I heal in relationship with others and the world. I feel better, and I play my part in a better world.

Maybe, as we heal the human societal climate, we heal the planetary climate?

lyeneba

25. Feeling

How does it feel to be alive? I've experienced a whole range - from my suicidal desperation on my 50th birthday, to a real sense, these days, of satisfaction often, and growing enjoyment. I can better accept, even welcome, all my feelings with more compassion - they all have a place in guiding me - whether fear, anger, sadness and other challenging and painful feelings, or more pleasurable, comfortable, wondrous or peaceful feelings. Often I feel a mix ... every feeling in the mix has something to tell me that I need to hear, about the past, the present and the way ahead. Unlove-illness distorts or traps my feelings in ways that mislead me - or numbs and deadens my feelings - whereas love opens my feelings into a flow of aliveness on a pathway of healing and life. I don't always distinguish love and unlove, I make mistakes, but overall life feels gradually better. How do we really want to feel?

love yes, extinction no, embracing being

26. War

Unlove generates destructive wars - whether inwardly between different parts of me, or outwardly between me and others ... and beyond, between other people, between communities or nations, between human and other living beings, between humans and planet. The awful result: needless suffering and needless death.

Love has only one war - a war against unlove while healing unlove-illness. Sometimes that may mean fighting someone or something that threatens to harm or kill us, but the battle is a battle of compassion for all involved, and where possible a battle of healing for all. Love has compassion for the aggressor in their unlove-illness, even when as a last resort love has to kill the aggressor in self-defence. Unlove's wars hasten extinction. Love's war on unlove is alive with peace and healing. Let's be warriors of love?

Iyeneba

27. Transforming

So much of the suffering in our world - whether through wars, or inner desperation, or whatever - is driven by (among other things) shame, blame, and guilt. These three engines of unlove offer no compassion for unlove-illness; they make us "bad" rather than recognising the need for healing. They cloud compassionate accountability. I am accountable for my choices; when I stole in the past, justice in court held me accountable. Today, when I feel shame, blame or guilt, I can let love gradually heal them into compassion, accountability and care with myself and others. Sometimes, if a person is dangerous, they must be confined. Not as a "prisoner" - but as an unlove-ill person needing healing, and for the safety and protection of them and others. Maybe love is transforming the toxic trio of shame, blame and guilt into compassionate, accountable caring in our healing world?

love yes, extinction no, embracing being

28. Sense

Love makes sense. Unlove makes no sense,
though it can seem to make sense.

Unlove-illness distorts sense. It puts a toxic filter on what I perceive, whether through my outer senses in what I see, hear, smell, taste, touch, or within myself through my bodily sense, emotional sense, and mental sense. Which then means my inner choices towards myself and outer choices in the world don't come from sense, even if they seem to. In the end this alienation from sense deadens my vitality, I become less alive, feel less alive. Love offers me compassion in this. I need healing, not punishing. I learned the 'sense' of unlove in a suffering family and culture of much unlove, of insufficient love. Love gradually restores sense - including the fabulous sense of aliveness that can maybe stop mass extinction and heal our world?

Iyeneba

29. Evolution

As well as the unlove of my upbringing, unlove-illness came to me genetically through age-old evolutionary imperatives for human survival. In today's world, these old human imperatives have morphed into the mis-evolution now threatening the survival of humanity. Traits that once served survival have become - in the changed circumstances of modern times - liabilities causing mass extinction and potential human extinction.

Yet love, too, is part of our evolutionary story and present reality. The love in our genes can evolve beyond genetic unlove - through a social and cultural evolution of more loving ways of being and living. These make us feel better and more alive. Extinction is evolution's ultimate challenge - evolutionary death - and love is rising to meet the challenge. As we evolve in real aliveness through growing love, maybe life can feel so much better?

love yes, extinction no, embracing being

30. Spiral

Sometimes it feels like we're doomed to spiral into ever worse mass extinction of species, heading towards human extinction too. The climate crisis, deforestation, pandemics, droughts, floods, fires, pollution, nuclear weapons, food insecurity, social division, military warfare - all these and more could engulf us. This is the legacy of unlove. Yet there is a growing legacy of love, a spiral of healing, in which I can play my small part along with others playing their small parts, as together we turn the spiral of extinction into a spiral of aliveness on this beautiful blue-green dot in the cosmos - planet Earth - a living world of burgeoning life for humans and other living beings - for eons to come - even as we maybe build or find other worlds, too, in our universe ... with love?

Iyeneba

31. Cosmos

When human beings journey further into our universe to build or find other living worlds, will we be fleeing a dying planet sick with unlove, or a thriving planet healing with love, a home to which we could return?

Of course, one day Earth will die, engulfed by the dying sun in billions of years, or maybe before that for another reason. I just hope it won't be humans who kill Earth. I can participate with others as we channel our human creativity for our world to survive and thrive, beautifully alive, even as we venture into the cosmos.

Maybe we will encounter other beings and worlds ... other universes ... a multiverse ... and more, that we as yet have no inkling of? Will we cause unlove-illness to grow in the cosmos, or will we evolve in growing love?

love yes, extinction no, embracing being

32. Intelligence

Unlove isn't the intelligent option, even when it gives me the illusion of being 'intelligent'. Unlove-illness clouds true intelligence and fosters harmful pseudo-intelligence that leads further into extinction, whether gradual inner living death, or dying community, or species death. Real intelligence makes us more alive.

Now our innate intelligence is being augmented with artificial intelligence - will we infect AI with more unlove or increasingly nurture it with love as a complementary intelligence to our own?

As individuals, we can link our personal intelligence into community intelligence and planetary intelligence - and one day maybe join with 'alien' intelligence in healing unlove-illness and vibrantly spreading love in our galaxy and universe?

Iyeneba

33. Time

My time offers me a tremendous opportunity to be part of a healing of unlove through growing love - both with myself and in community with others in our world. I can spend my time in ways that make me more alive, participating in our shared aliveness on amazing Earth.

Unlove deadens life as time goes by, deadens the aliveness in each moment.

I can have compassion for unlove-illness in me and others, and understand that it's not about perfection, but about getting better.

Pain, whether in me or others, can be met with compassion and care. And while time in each moment brings us towards our dying (whenever, however, and whatever that may be) here now, day by day, we are maybe growingly alive with love?

love yes, extinction no, embracing being

34. Children

The choices we make now, impact children - directly or indirectly - and for generations to come. As unlove-illness heals, as love grows, we can create a better world for children now and in the future. A better world for children is a better world for adults too, and for the other living beings we share this planet with. A world not of hastening mass extinction, but of evolving abundant aliveness. Serious. Fun.

Among all the children, I need to remember the child I once was and still carry inside myself ... me as a baby soon to be born, then birthing, newborn, growing, toddler, child, teen ... raised more with unlove than love in a suffering, unlove-ill family and culture - yet with love too, the love that has threaded through human history amid unlove, the love that heals inner children, that loves all children and all of us beings on Earth?

Iyeneba

35. Weaving

All the threads of love can weave together in a fabric of healing - inwardly within us and outwardly in our world. Unlove's tangled threads can - as unlove-illness heals - be unpicked, transformed, rewoven within the fabric of love.

As my unlove-illness heals bit by bit, love grows within me and in community with others. I can weave my personal threads among our community threads and planetary threads of growing aliveness. In doing this my aliveness grows too. It can be a win-win-win: personally, and for community, and for the planet.

We can feel better - including through our compassion and care for suffering whether in ourselves or others. Mortal and alive - we can weave-weave-weave … win-win-win … www … warm-wondrous-well?

love yes, extinction no, embracing being

36. Space

As I write this book, sometimes the words flow, at other times I feel stuck. The page is a space where I can bring language. I need to allow myself space to learn and grow, to make mistakes, to try things, then other things, to breathe, to be. Space! The page-space shifts and changes until it finally becomes what you are reading.

There is perhaps a kind of virtual space that you and I share as reader and writer. At the same time, we each have our own space.

All of us have personal space, within us and around us - yet our personal spaces meet in our sharing the space of our world - and perhaps sharing, too, the prospects beyond Earth, in outer space. All space for love?

Iyeneba

37. Compassion

Sometimes unlove can seem like love to me. One of the many symptoms of unlove-illness is misperceiving unlove as 'love'. Somewhere deep within me there is a quest and hunger for love, that was hijacked by unlove in my formative years as a baby and child. I attached to unlove when what I really needed was an attachment with love. I had no choice, just as those who came before me were once babies and children who had no choice.

Healing gives me choice. It starts with compassion for myself and others. The attachment to unlove is rooted in wounds, from one generation to the next - a long, long history of wounding - and compassion somehow has a way of opening wounds so that love can come in and heal them. Love hates and stops unlove while healing unlove-illness and loving us all?

love yes, extinction no, embracing being

38. Matter

When I'm dying ... at the end(?) of my life, or the beginning(?) of a new phase in my existence, or whatever(?) ... at the furthest edge, at any rate, of my time in this form on Earth ... and if I'm not overwhelmed by pain, or maybe chaos ... who knows ... as I face what we call 'death', the thing I'll care about, I'm sure, is love and the healing of unlove-illness in our world and maybe beyond ... this is what will matter to me ... love ... all of us and our planet, alive, in a cosmos that perhaps beckons us to further aliveness in other worlds, other universes, and maybe other realms beyond time and space? ... yet right here, right now, in this realm on Earth where I live today, I can do my bit to counter extinction - the gradual personal inner living death and the outer dying of community, linked with accelerating mass extinction - that maybe we can stop! Healing ourselves and our world. Love?

lyeneba

39. Relating

I exist in relationship - whether I'm aware of it or not (sometimes I am aware, sometimes not, i.e. unlove-ill) - in relationship with everyone and everything in our world and universe, as well as my inner world and universe. I am a relating being, among other relating beings, in an interrelating web of life - alive. Unlove-illness distorts my relating, turning it towards extinction - inwardly and outwardly - a slow living death. Love compassionately recognises and accepts my unlove-illness for healing, embraces the unlove-ill parts of me, gradually restoring their capacity to relate - my capacity to relate with myself, others, our world ... including through this book, relating with you.

Here we are - alive - in a world alive and healing with love?

love yes, extinction no, embracing being

40. Language

Words and language have evolved since humans first communicated ... even before humans - given how other living beings on Earth have words and language too, whether vocalised, signed or however. As I write these words and you read them, your 'here and now' and my 'here and now' are separate - yet somehow words bridge the separation and connect us. Words can build bridges - and undermine or destroy bridges. The language of unlove, even when it seems to bridge, in reality unbridges, whether inwardly with myself or outwardly with others. Words of unbridging drive extinction - the slow inner living death, and the dying of community, and mass extinction. Silence, too, can bridge or unbridge. And music, images, signs, touch .... can bridge or unbridge. Love's language - in and beyond words - bridges our aliveness?

Iyeneba

41. Creating

In unlove-illness, power without love 'creates' more unlove; as does vulnerability without love. In healing, love brings vulnerability and power together, through caring; love's vulnerability, power and care combine to create more love. Unlove's 'creativity' distorts power, exploits vulnerability, loses care - this isn't real creativity. Love is real creativity. In the mix of love and unlove, creativity too is a mix. Maybe the creativity-mix is shifting growingly from unlove to love, as we and our world heal creatively. Personal creating is interdependent with community creating. Together, personal and community creating can maybe interweave with planetary creating, saving our world. As we evolve, maybe Earth's creativities can interweave with other planetary creativities ... galactic creativities ... cosmic creativities ... each and all of us ... creating with love?

love yes, extinction no, embracing being

42. Lyeneba

LYENEBA - Love Yes, Extinction No, Embracing Being Alive ... the acronym lyeneba is a word that helps me live life. A versatile word: it can be a noun, a verb, an adjective, an adverb ... and more...?

Noun - lyeneba is a way of life for me.

Verb - I can lyeneba to the best of my ability.

Adjective - I aim to live a lyeneba life.

Adverb - I want to live as lyeneba as I can.

Every choice I make in my inner and outer world is either unloving, loving, or most often a mix. Every choice, great or small, ultimately either harms or helps lyeneba. No undue pressure, though! Mistakes happen. And there are sometimes confusions, uncertainties. Yet maybe we are getting better at living with compassion, clarity and care with ourselves, others and our world. Maybe as unlove-illness heals, there can be less needless pain and needless death, more love, more aliveness, more lyeneba?

43. Love

I can't define love, or pin it down. I experience it, yet don't always know what exactly I'm experiencing. Sometimes, what I took to be love turns out to include at least some unlove; I have misperceptions about love, which are gradually healing. But I'm not sure I'll ever be entirely free of misperceptions in this life. I live in a mix of unlove and love, and I'm healing - growingly discovering love alongside others, as together and individually we open a way or ways. Is there another life beyond death? I don't know. Perhaps ... whether as 'me', a being among beings within maybe universal being(s); or 'me-less' as part of an ongoing aliveness and loving wholeness of being; or somehow both 'me' and 'me-less'; or...? Will you and I and all of us 'meet' again? ... Meanwhile, here now on Earth, maybe we can increase our personal wellbeing, our community wellbeing, our shared planetary wellbeing, maybe we can save and heal ourselves and our world with growing love, maybe we and future generations can survive, thrive, be really alive, maybe we can stop the mass extinction of species, stabilise the climate, nurture life, maybe we can eradicate war and resolve conflicts peacefully, maybe we can truly care for ourselves and other living beings, end needless suffering and needless death, alleviate unavoidable suffering, ease the experience of dying, maybe we can create a better life for all, and all feel better about life, maybe we can be happier along with all our feelings, maybe we can be in a compassionate, 'imperfect' yet real process of healing unlove-illness, stopping unlove, experiencing love more, maybe we can, maybe we will, maybe we are already making this possible, making it true, taking our place in a love story unfolding on Earth, in the cosmos, within and around us, and beyond?

(Not) The End

What next?

Maybe we're finding a way...

I wish you all the best with your way...

I seem to be gradually discovering my way...

Your way and my way can be part of humanity's way and Earth's way. Our way - of many ways.

Thank you for reading this book.

If you liked it, please spread the word and help other people find it. You could:

- leave a rating and review where you purchased it, and maybe elsewhere too.
- talk to others about it.
- gift it to people.

> Shall we lyeneba?!

Acknowledgements

This book benefitted immeasurably through support and insight, together with vital human connection, from:

Kim and Sinclair Macleod of Indie Authors World

Jodene Antoniou of Capital Captions

Dominic Stuart

Louisa Parsons

The Alliance of Independent Authors (who, among many other benefits, introduced me to Indie Authors World)

along with others who contributed to this book indirectly, also through vital human connection:

The folks who help with my care

Many friends

My sibs and extended family

Thank you all so much!

www.ingramcontent.com/pod-product-compliance
Lightning Source LLC
Chambersburg PA
CBHW020133130526
44590CB00040B/606